– THE UNTOLD STORY OF –

JOHN P. PARKER

UNDERGROUND RAILROAD CONDUCTOR

BY DR. ARTIKA R. TYNER

CAPSTONE PRESS
a capstone imprint

Published by Capstone Press, an imprint of Capstone
1710 Roe Crest Drive, North Mankato, Minnesota 56003
capstonepub.com

Library of Congress Cataloging-in-Publication Data
Names: Tyner, Artika R., author.
Title: The untold story of John P. Parker : Underground Railroad conductor / by Dr. Artika R. Tyner.
Other titles: Underground Railroad conductor
Description: North Mankato, Minnesota : Capstone Press, an imprint of Capstone, [2024] | Series: First but forgotten | Includes bibliographical references and index. | Audience: Ages 8 to 11 | Audience: Grades 4–6 | Summary: "Most people have heard about Harriet Tubman helping enslaved people emancipate themselves. But there were many others who helped enslaved people gain their freedom through the Underground Railroad. John P. Parker was one of them, helping enslaved people cross the Ohio River to freedom. With key biographical information and related historical events, this Capstone Captivate book uncovers Parker's remarkable story"—Provided by publisher.
Identifiers: LCCN 2022051090 (print) | LCCN 2022051091 (ebook) |
  ISBN 9781669016182 (hardcover) | ISBN 9781669016137 (paperback) | ISBN 9781669016144 (ebook pdf)
  ISBN 9781669016168 (kindle edition) | ISBN 9781669016175 (epub)
Subjects: LCSH: Parker, John P., 1827–1900—Juvenile literature. | Underground Railroad—Ohio—Juvenile literature. | African American abolitionists—Ohio—Biography—Juvenile literature. | Abolitionists—Ohio—Biography—Juvenile literature. | Freed persons—Biography—Juvenile literature. | Ripley (Ohio)—Biography—Juvenile literature.
Classification: LCC E450 .P239 2024 (print) | LCC E450 (ebook) | DDC 973.7/115092 [B]—dc23/eng/20221026
LC record available at https://lccn.loc.gov/2022051090
LC ebook record available at https://lccn.loc.gov/2022051091

Editorial Credits
Editor: Ericka Smith; Designer: Kayla Rossow; Media Researcher: Svetlana Zhurkin; Production Specialist: Katy LaVigne

Image Credits
Alamy: North Wind Picture Archives, 7, 11, Tom Uhlman, 26, 28; Bridgeman Images: © Bristol Museums, Galleries & Archives/Bequest of William Jerdone Braikenridge, 1908, 9, © Keith Rocco, All Rights Reserved 2023, cover, 19, © New York Public Library, 23; Courtesy of the Kentucky Heritage Council/State Historic Preservation Office/Photo by Catherine Bache: 21; Courtesy of the Ohio History Connection, #AL01028: 27; Library of Congress: 25; Shutterstock: Everett Collection, 5, Julia Khimich (background), cover (right) and throughout, Nadegda Rozova (background), cover (left) and throughout; U.S. Patent and Trademark Office: 15; Wikimedia: Nyttend, 13; XNR Productions: 17

Direct Quotation
Page 29, from *His Promised Land: The Autobiography of John P. Parker, Former Slave and Conductor on the Underground Railroad*, by John P. Parker. New York: W.W. Norton. Company, 1998.

All internet sites appearing in back matter were available and accurate when this book was sent to press.

Printed and bound in China. 5379

TABLE OF CONTENTS

INTRODUCTION
Early Abolitionist 4

CHAPTER ONE
Born into Slavery 6

CHAPTER TWO
The Promise of Freedom 10

CHAPTER THREE
Becoming a Conductor 16

CHAPTER FOUR
Legacy of a Freedom Fighter 28

Glossary 30
Read More 31
Internet Sites 31
Index 32
About the Author 32

Words in **bold** are in the glossary.

EARLY ABOLITIONIST

John P. Parker was born into slavery. But he believed freedom was a **birthright**. He thought no one should own another human being. His passion for justice led him to not only buy his freedom, but also help others gain theirs.

Parker was a **conductor** on the Underground Railroad in Ohio. He would cross the Ohio River into Kentucky to help enslaved people gain their freedom. This work was very dangerous, and Parker could have been imprisoned or killed. But he took the risk time and time again. Between 1845 and 1865, he helped free hundreds of enslaved people.

Parker was part of an important network of people who helped enslaved people gain their freedom through the Underground Railroad. You have probably heard about conductors like Harriet Tubman. But others—like Parker—often remain unknown. This is his story.

Abolitionists of All Kinds

Parker joined a community of dedicated **abolitionists** who fought to end slavery. Some helped enslaved people **emancipate** themselves. Others used their skills—such as writing and public speaking—to raise awareness about how cruel slavery was and encourage others to help bring an end to the practice. In 1829, David Walker wrote *Appeal to the Colored Citizens of the World* and challenged those who were enslaved to fight for their freedom. In 1847, Frederick Douglass founded the abolitionist newspaper the *North Star* to share his message of freedom across the United States. Sojourner Truth helped advocate for abolition by sharing the horrors of slavery experienced by women.

Frederick Douglass

CHAPTER ONE

BORN INTO SLAVERY

Parker was born in 1827 in Norfolk, Virginia. His mother was Black and enslaved, which meant he would be enslaved too. His father was white. At 8 years old, he was taken away from his mother. He was forced to walk nearly 100 miles (161 kilometers) from Norfolk to Richmond, Virginia. There, he would be sold.

During this journey, Parker witnessed firsthand the violence of slavery. He saw an **enslaver** beat an elderly man that Parker was chained to so badly that he killed him.

Six months after Parker had arrived in Richmond, he was sold to a doctor as a house servant. He had to walk across several states to the doctor's home in Mobile, Alabama. During that trip, he was shackled and bound by chain to other enslaved people. About 400 women, men, and children were chained together.

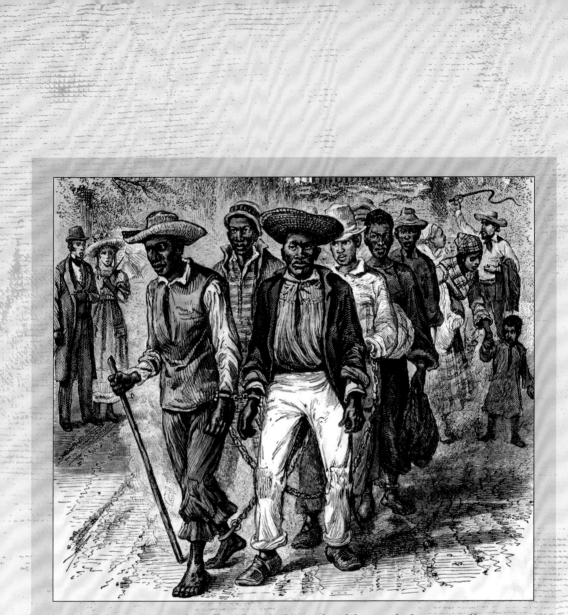

A large group of enslaved people in shackles and chains walking along a dirt road

In Mobile, Parker's enslaver knew he could make more money by having Parker work for other businesses. At 12 years old, Parker started his first **apprenticeship**. He worked with a **plasterer**.

One day, the plasterer beat Parker so badly that he ended up in the hospital. He left the hospital determined to free himself from enslavement. He came up with a plan to escape to the North, where he could be free.

When Parker tried to emancipate himself, he was caught in New Orleans, Louisiana. He was forced to return to the doctor in Mobile. But the failed attempt did not stop Parker from seeking his freedom.

FACT In 1833, Alabama made it illegal to teach an enslaved person or a free person of color how to read or write. Although illegal, the doctor's sons taught Parker how to read and write.

Plasterers applying a finish to the wall of a building

CHAPTER TWO

THE PROMISE OF FREEDOM

After he was forced to return to his enslaver, Parker started a new apprenticeship in iron molding. He often had conflict with managers, and the doctor worried that this was a pattern that would continue to create trouble. He decided to sell Parker as a field worker.

Parker didn't want to work in the fields, so he convinced one of the doctor's patients, Elizabeth Ryder, to purchase him.

After Ryder purchased him, Parker worked in a **foundry**—where metal is molded into shapes. He worked seven days a week and saved any extra money he made to buy his freedom.

After about two years, Parker had saved enough to buy his freedom. It cost $1,800. In 1845, at the age of 18, he finally became a free man.

Ironworkers in the 1800s

Once free, Parker moved north. The North represented a better future. He could use the skills he learned as an apprentice to work for himself.

Parker first lived in Indiana. Later, he moved to Cincinnati, Ohio. In 1848, he opened a general store. He married Miranda Boulden on May 12, 1848. They would have seven children together.

Around 1850, Parker and his family moved to Ripley, Ohio. There, he built his own foundry. He employed others in the community, Black and white alike. And he invented new tools and machinery.

Parker's house in Ripley, Ohio

When he was 18 years old, Parker developed his first invention while working at a foundry in Mobile. He created a clod-smashing machine. Farmers use it to prepare the ground before planting seeds. He shared it with his supervisor, who took the machine. Parker never saw his invention again. Parker told the owner of the foundry, but his supervisor claimed that he had designed the tool—not Parker.

Despite this setback, Parker continued to create new tools. Once in Ripley, he created many inventions at his foundry and **patented** them. He created a soil **pulverizer,** which breaks down soil in preparation for new fields and driveways. He also invented a tobacco press, which presses tobacco leaves together to release their flavors.

FACT Parker was one of only a few Black people who had patents in the 1800s. Only 55 Black people had more than one patent in 1901.

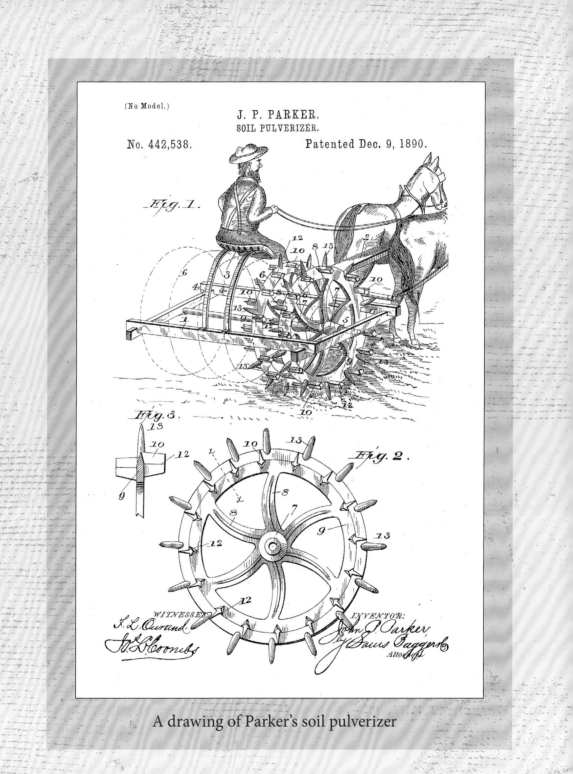

A drawing of Parker's soil pulverizer

BECOMING A CONDUCTOR

Not long after Parker had purchased his own freedom, he began to help others. His first rescue was in 1845 while in Cincinnati. A free man asked him to help two enslaved girls. Parker initially refused. But the man was persistent.

Eventually the man convinced Parker to join him. But it was Parker alone who brought the girls from Maysville, Kentucky, to freedom in Ripley. This rescue inspired him to move to Ripley and focus more on serving as a conductor on the Underground Railroad.

To do this work, Parker crossed the Ohio River by boat in the middle of the night. He then traveled on land for miles to rescue his **passengers** and bring them to **stations**.

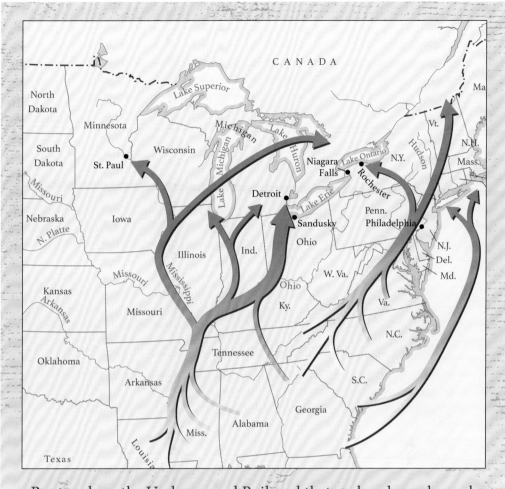

Routes along the Underground Railroad that enslaved people used to gain their freedom

FACT The Ohio River marked a border between states where people were enslaved, like Kentucky, and free states, like Ohio. Many enslaved people crossed the Ohio River to freedom.

As a conductor, Parker witnessed the courage and determination of enslaved people seeking their birthright. During one journey, Parker helped a husband and wife who could not swim safely cross the Ohio River. The wife lay on a log while her husband used his legs to paddle them across the Ohio River.

Parker also witnessed enslaved people show great compassion for one another. On one trip, Parker had only a small boat. More people were waiting than could fit in the boat. And they didn't have much time before they would be caught. One man decided to stay while his wife got on the boat. But another man gave up his seat so that the couple could stay together. The man who gave up his seat was caught before he was able to cross the Ohio River.

Enslaved people crossing a river by boat

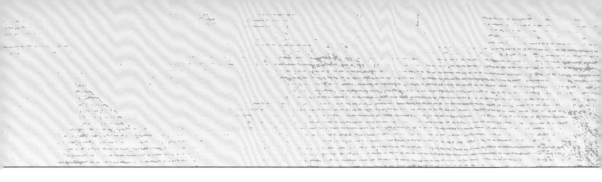

Parker's most dangerous mission was saving a couple and their child in Kentucky. The baby was kept in their enslaver's home, at the foot of the enslaver's bed. He did this to keep the parents from running away—they would not leave without their child.

In the middle of the night, Parker went into the enslaver's bedroom. He saw guns on the nightstand. Carefully, he grabbed the baby. As he was leaving the room, the enslaver woke up and bumped the nightstand. The guns fell to the floor.

The house in Dover, Kentucky, where Parker rescued the baby

Parker darted out of the bedroom with the baby. The enslaver fired at him, but the bullet flew above Parker's head.

Parker ran at full speed toward the river with the baby in his arms. The baby's parents ran alongside him. Once they reached Ripley, Parker sent them on the next leg of their journey along the Underground Railroad.

But the family's enslaver pursued Parker. He went to Parker's home in Ripley with two other men. They demanded he return the enslaver's "property"—the family that had escaped. Parker allowed them to inspect his home. The enslaver was angry when he could not find the couple and the baby. But Parker was proud that he had saved the entire family.

Conductors on the Underground Railroad
helping a family free themselves

Being a conductor on the Underground Railroad put Parker's life at risk. He was breaking the law and could face prison or even death. But those risks did not stop him. Instead, Parker tried to keep his identity secret by working at night and completing his missions by himself. At one point, though, there was a $1,000 reward for capturing him in Kentucky—dead or alive.

After the Civil War began in 1861, Parker's work expanded to include recruiting soldiers for the Union Army. He helped recruit Black men for the military. He also helped hundreds of enslaved people escape to the North and join the Union Army.

FACT There are no known photographs of John P. Parker.

A Woman of Many Achievements

Harriet Tubman was a well-known conductor on the Underground Railroad. Between 1849 and 1860, she helped emancipate dozens of enslaved people and earned the nickname "Moses" because of her commitment to freeing her people.

During the Civil War, she was the first woman to lead a major military operation. In 1863, she led 150 Black Union soldiers in the Combahee Ferry Raid in South Carolina. During the raid, they saved 700 enslaved people. She also served as a nurse and a spy for the Union Army.

After the Civil War, Parker continued to build his businesses. In 1865, he and his business partner bought a new foundry and a blacksmith shop. By 1870, he was the twenty-seventh person on a list of the wealthiest people in Ripley, Ohio.

In the 1870s and 1880s, many businesses were forced to close because of **economic** problems in the country. While Parker faced challenges, it helped that he owned businesses in more than one industry. As one industry struggled, he could rely on his other businesses.

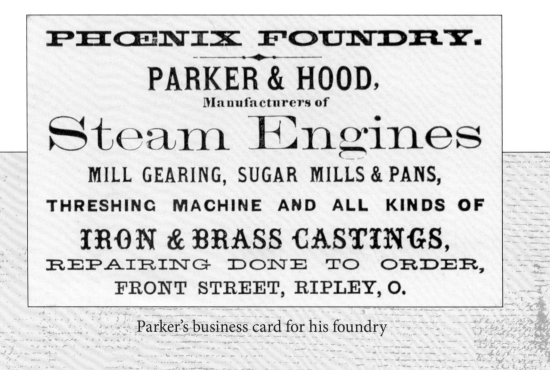

Parker's business card for his foundry

At home, Parker taught his children to love learning. He sent all his children to college, and many of them later became educators.

Parker also continued to serve his community in Ohio. One way he did this was by mentoring young Black people.

Parker died in Ripley on January 30, 1900. But he left behind a legacy of remarkable achievements.

Some think that the man on the far right in this 1892 photograph might be John P. Parker.

CHAPTER FOUR

LEGACY OF A FREEDOM FIGHTER

In 1997, Parker's home in Ripley became a historic landmark and a museum. The museum documents his life history, including his work as a conductor on the Underground Railroad. Three of his inventions are displayed there as well.

Parker's house and soil pulverizer

Parker's life serves as an inspiration to us all to challenge injustice. Parker said, "I know slavery's curse was not pain of the body, but the pain of the soul." And he risked his freedom and his life to help others free their souls from its curse. His determination is a reminder to fight the injustices we see however we can.

Parker Tells His Story

After the Civil War, Parker was interviewed by journalist Frank Moody Gregg for an autobiography. The interview documented his work as a conductor on the Underground Railroad. The book is titled *His Promised Land: The Autobiography of John P. Parker, Former Slave and Conductor on the Underground Railroad*. The money from the book's sales now supports the John P. Parker Historical Society.

GLOSSARY

abolitionist (ab-uh-LIH-shuhn-ist)—a person who worked to end slavery

apprenticeship (uh-PREN-tiss-ship)—an arrangement in which someone works for a skilled person, often for a basic wage, in order to learn that person's skills

birthright (BURTH-rahyt)—a right everyone has at birth

conductor (kuhn-DUHK-tuhr)—a person who helped enslaved people on the Underground Railroad

economic (ek-uh-NOM-ik)—having to do with a country's money and resources

emancipate (ih-MAN-suh-payt)—to free from slavery

enslaver (in-SLAYV-uhr)—a person who holds another in bondage against their will

foundry (FOUN-dree)—a place for melting and shaping metal

passenger (PASS-uhn-jur)—an enslaved person who uses the Underground Railroad to free themselves

patent (PAT-uhnt)—to get a legal document giving someone sole rights to make or sell a product

plasterer (PLASS-tur-uhr)—someone who applies plaster, a hard substance made of lime, sand, and water, to surfaces

pulverizer (PUHL-vuh-riz-uhr)—a tool used for grinding

station (STAY-shuhn)—a hiding place on the Underground Railroad

READ MORE

Enz, Tammy. *Science on the Underground Railroad.* North Mankato, MN: Capstone, 2023.

Messner, Kate and Gwendolyn Hooks. *The Underground Railroad.* New York: Random House, 2022.

Platt, Christine. *The Story of Harriet Tubman: A Biography Book for New Readers.* Emeryville, CA: Rockridge Press, 2020.

INTERNET SITES

Britannica Kids: Harriet Tubman
kids.britannica.com/kids/article/Harriet-Tubman/353874

Britannica Kids: Underground Railroad
kids.britannica.com/kids/article/Underground-Railroad/353882

National Geographic Kids: The Underground Railroad
kids.nationalgeographic.com/history/article/the-underground-railroad

INDEX

Alabama, 6, 8

Appeal to the Colored Citizens of the World, 5

Boulden, Miranda, 12

Cincinnati, Ohio, 12, 16
Civil War, 24, 25, 26, 29
Combahee Ferry Raid, 25

Douglass, Frederick, 5
Dover, Kentucky, 21

Gregg, Frank Moody, 29

His Promised Land: The Autobiography of John P. Parker, Former Slave and Conductor on the Underground Railroad, 29

Kentucky, 4, 16, 17, 20, 21, 24

Maysville, Kentucky, 16
Mobile, Alabama, 6, 8, 14

New Orleans, Louisiana, 8
Norfolk, Virginia, 6
North Star, 5

Ohio, 4, 12, 13, 17, 26, 27
Ohio River, 4, 16, 17, 18

Richmond, Virginia, 6
Ripley, Ohio, 12, 13, 14, 16, 22, 26, 27, 28
Ryder, Elizabeth, 10

Sojourner Truth, 5
South Carolina, 25

Tubman, Harriet, 4, 25

Union Army, 24, 25

Walker, David, 5

ABOUT THE AUTHOR

Dr. Artika R. Tyner is a passionate educator, award-winning author, a civil rights attorney, a sought-after speaker, and an advocate for justice. She lives in Saint Paul, Minnesota, and is the founder of the Planting People Growing Justice Leadership Institute.